Get Your Home Office Organized

Get Your Home Office Organized

Cut the Clutter
And Watch Your Productivity Soar!

By Cynthia Charleen Alexander

Copyright © 2015 by Cynthia Charlene Alexander
ISBN: 978-1-937988-23-4

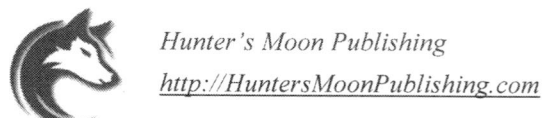

Hunter's Moon Publishing
http://HuntersMoonPublishing.com

Disclaimer

The opinions expressed in this book are not a guarantee of results, because the results will be determined by your efforts and decisions. Each person's experience will be different.

The ideas in this book are not meant to take the place of legal, tax, medical or other professional advice. If you need that type of advice, please seek a qualified professional.

My wish for you: "Go forth and prosper"

As the purchaser of this book you are entitled to special training through my website. To receive this information and access to the additional materials visit http://GetYourHomeOfficeOrganized.com.

Right away, you will receive a special report on organizing your car as a mobile office, as well as examples and resources for the furniture and online tools mentioned in the book.

I want you to be successful and this will help to ensure that you have every possible tool at your disposal. Follow me and let's get organized for business!

Contents

Foreword

What a pleasure and an honor to write the foreword for my friend and colleague Cynthia Alexander! When I first met Cynthia a few years ago, she was well into her journey of living a more organized life. I remember visiting her home for the first time and admiring the way she had eliminated a lot of the types of clutter that can so easily accumulate over years of raising three children and having a full-time corporate career and a big city commute.

During my visit, I noticed that her office, her kitchen, and her living room were organized. Even her closets, her pantry, and her linen closet were organized. I'm not talking about spaces that were sterile or cold or uncomfortably plain. I could tell that she was a real person with a life and grandchildren, someone who really lives in her space. But things were neat and comfortable and accessible... Very livable.

As a coach who helps people discover their next career steps, I'm always fascinated when people pursue a new career direction. I knew that Cynthia hadn't been a professional organizer in her corporate career. When I asked her about how she had become a professional organizer, I was surprised by her answer.

She told me that she had not always been organized, that she wasn't like so many professional organizers who are naturally neat and organized. She told me that it was only in recent years that she had learned how to live a more organized life. I was fascinated and inspired by her story.

I loved hearing about how she is now able to help other people with their organizing. Whether it is a stay–at–home parent with a home-based business, a busy professional who needs high-tech office space at home or someone near retirement who wants to start a small business after their primary career, Cynthia knows ways to help them with a home office that will work well for them.

When she told me that she was writing this book, I was very excited because now her method and approach to organizing can help even more people. I appreciate the way she shares ideas and approaches that are practical and workable in the real world.

So, if you work from home part-time or full-time, this book is for you. You've taken the first step by getting this book. You don't have to try to organize your whole house to see results. Just start with your home office. Whether you work at a corner of the family dinner table, or you have a separate large room for your office, getting your home office space organized will energize you and increase your productivity.

I encourage you to dive in, follow Cynthia's guidance, and reap the wonderful rewards!

Leslie Cardinal

To my mother Jean Cook who always encouraged me and told me that I can do anything I set my mind to do. Thanks for your ongoing love.

PREFACE

"How you do anything in your life is how you do everything." –Dr. Phil

I'm so glad that you've decided that it is time to make a change when it comes to organizing your life! I know that my world would be a mess if I didn't use all of the organization techniques that you are about to learn. Let's start by talking about how this book came to be and why I am so passionate about clearing out clutter and organizing. You see, I haven't always been this way! I lived most of my life being disorganized and surrounded by excess.

I turned my life around, got organized and broke away from the habit of procrastination. For me, and most of you, clutter really is about postponed decisions. When you come in to the house and put your stuff on the kitchen counter or toss your things on the couch, you are simply postponing the decision to put it all up. The clutter soon begins to accumulate and suddenly the clean and clear kitchen counter is full of paper, books and perhaps a sack of groceries waiting to be put away.

The result is clutter. This is not just the kind of clutter that is merely in the way – it is the kind of clutter that weighs your mind down. Your brain becomes cluttered, constantly reminding you of the reminder of things you still need to do before the day is done; like clean up that clutter! As a business owner and nester, I have found that my mental energy keeps being diverted to thinking about all of the things that I need to do before I can settle down and work on my business. If I ignore the stuff, my concentration is still interrupted by the nagging thought that after I finish, much more is left to do before I can relax and enjoy my day.

I don't think that anyone sets the goal of being distracted. I can't remember a time that I heard someone say, "I hope that I can find something to distract me today and prevent me from being productive and prosperous." By reading this book, you will discover ways that will reveal what type of clutter is in your life, why it's there, and how decluttering will help you enjoy your business more.

Clutter doesn't have to be present in all areas of your life to be a distraction. It may sneak into just a few areas, lay quiet, and pounce when the time is right. When I worked in the corporate world, I was able to keep my desk organized. I developed a routine that I followed to process the work on my desk so that each task was completed successfully and on time. In fact, I was recognized for accuracy and productivity. When I left that position, I was actually in charge of correcting orders for the other team members in addition to my own workload!

However, that was not the case at home. In my home office, I felt out of control and scattered with too much that had been left undone. Little did I know, but this issue would open a new career that would enable me to reach out and share with others. In my 30 Day Plan, I will share some simple methods that will help you gain control of your clutter and kick it to the curb. As you discover what is holding you back from productivity, good things will start to happen almost overnight.

I share my story with the hope you are able to take away some insights and helpful tips that you can apply to organizing your home office and increasing your productivity and enjoyment as an entrepreneur. When you organize and eliminate clutter, your business will grow and you will have greater opportunities for success and satisfaction in your business.

Take the time to discover the truth about clutter and disorganization and learn to apply actions that will help unlock the key to a well ordered life that is custom fit for you. Clutter is sneaky and will work its way into all areas of your life before you know it. For a home business, it is a silent killer.

INTRODUCTION

Anyone can make significant progress in getting their home office organized in 30 days or less by following the outline that you will find inside these pages. About 80% of people want to get their office organized but never do. The reason: it's too hard – until now.

When you attempt to do it all at once, the inspiration and energy run out before the job is completed. After a few attempts over the years, most people give up and resign themselves to never getting organized. This book contains the step by step process that I have used to complete an entire office in less than a month. You will discover how you can declutter and organize your office when done one step at a time.

We will start with Day 1 and clearing out the clutter. The excess stuff that people have is the biggest challenge to success and can jeopardize the entire project. It's hard to be successful on a project when you have trouble getting past the first week!

Day 2 finishes the clutter purge. As you work the plan, create your design and arrange your office so it is a place where you can work in comfort and peace. You will have the opportunity to learn new skills and techniques that can be applied in both your home and business. Whether you are a busy mother working during the times that the children are napping or working full time and pursuing a career, your contribution to the world is important. You have a message that only you can deliver. No one else can tell your message better than you can. So the saga continues through the 30 Day Plan that you will find at the book's end.

Today is the day to begin your journey from the chaos of clutter into an organized world of increased productivity. Make those minutes count. Does this sound like a message for you? Then read on…….

Chapter 1 – THE TRANSFORMATION BEGINS

"You must choose between the various alternatives in order to make the most of the time and energy we do have. We choose constantly in order to bring as much happiness as possible, while using up as little time and energy as possible."
Harry Browne

It was a warm summer day and my daughter was coming to spend the morning with me. I was looking forward to spending time chatting and perhaps even going out for a bite of lunch. It was not often that we got to spend an entire morning together. I was surprised when she came to the door with baskets and totes in hand. "Mom, we've been talking and we are embarrassed about all the stuff that you have piled up in the house. I have come to help you get control of the stuff". She and her two brothers had organized a "clutter intervention" and I was the addict!

I was both stunned and embarrassed because I didn't consider the stuff to be a problem. After all, the kitchen floors and even the bathrooms were always clean. I certainly would admit to having lots of bags and boxes in the closets, and sure, I had a few plastic tubs filled with fabric and crafting supplies. Yes, there were pictures stacked in corners. But, hey, that just makes a home looked lived in, right? Sometimes I would need to clear a spot up on the couch so that someone could sit down. Never had it occurred to me that it was a source of embarrassment for my children. These things represented our precious memories. At least, that's how I perceived it. Oh well, I've been wrong before!

That day began a new chapter of my life. We spent the morning organizing the bathroom. Baskets and boxes were used to separate and categorize everything from towels to lotions, cleaning supplies and hair curlers. I'm so grateful that she was brave enough to tell me that my clutter was an issue. Lots of stuff went out the door that day some to charity and some to the trash!

Why am I sharing this with you? When I want to learn about a topic, I seek out someone who has experience; someone who has walked the walk not just talked the talk. Let me tell you, clutter and organizing is the subject in which I have much experience. It's not my proudest moment but perhaps it is the most revealing.

Making organizing simple and convenient is the first step towards creating a plan that will work on the long term. If it is easy to do, then that encourages compliance with the PLAN. No one can make the decision for you. The process is similar to losing weight. Only you can make the decision and decide what works for your way of doing things.

Here's a tip: You should always start with a plan that fits your wants, needs and lifestyle.

Don't be tempted to copy from someone else. Some people are only comfortable when the entire house looks like a page from a home magazine. Others are quite comfortable with a more relaxed plan. You can certainly use suggestions and input from others to find the plan that works for you. This information should help model a plan that is custom right fit for you and those around you. I like to take the best ideas and adapt them to my client needs.

Let's begin to find the tools that will help you discover a path towards gaining control of your time. This will give you more opportunities to grow your business and achieve your goals. Make a promise to yourself that you will persevere to organize your home office, find your best self and learn to soar. Raise your right hand and swear.......!

Chapter 2- DECLUTTER

"I think we all have a little voice inside us that will guide us... if we shut out all the noise and clutter from our lives and listen to that voice, it will tell us the right thing to do."
~Christopher Reeve

There is no reason to even begin organizing before you've decluttered. And before you've decluttered, take a moment to figure out exactly why it is that you do what you do. For me, I grew up in a busy home where we seemed to always be on our way to school, church or other activities. Life was never dull. As a busy teenager I would rush in, grab a bite to eat, and then rush out the door again.

My room was also the laundry area. There was not a door to my room, so I never had the privacy of having my own space all to myself. – Did I mention that it was also the back door of the house? Great view – but was not having my very own room where I could shut the door and have everything to myself.

I went off to college where I shared a small room with a roommate. With two girls in such a tiny space, we were bursting at the seams. We had clothes, books and lots of food stacked under tables and on the floor. The cafeteria food tasted like …cafeteria food…so we kept our own grocery in our little room.

The next stage in my life brought marriage and a family with all the responsibility that comes with it.

Our house was not large, so as our family grew so did the amount of stuff. Then I had teenagers and all the activity that comes with school, church, band and jobs. Since I worked full time, volunteered and fed a family of five, there never seemed to be enough hours in the day to get everything done.

Things began to accumulate in closets and storage. We seemed to be bursting at the seams! Suddenly I was a single parent trying to hold a family together and keep life as normal as possible. With two children in college and one in junior high, I was living in a world of overwhelm.

Finally, I packed up and moved to Dallas where we could get a fresh start. Living in an apartment was crowded and we still seemed to have lots of stuff. I don't know exactly where we crossed the line, but it began to resemble life in a closet full of things.

The stuff followed us as I bought my first home as a single mom. We had more space again, but you know the saying "no matter how much space you have, the stuff expands to fill it" and fill it we did. Boxes and bags were in closets and corners. Plastic tubs were stacked 2 or 3 high in the corner of my office. This was the site of the "clutter intervention".

A 2014 article written by Melinda Beck in the Wall Street Journal talks about the psychology of clutter and why people hold on to things and don't organize. One reason states that chronic disorganization can be a symptom of Attention Deficit Hyperactivity Disorder, Obsessive-Compulsive Disorder and dementia. Each of these can cause difficulty with planning, focusing and making decisions like when to throw something away and where to file things.

Simon Rego, director of psychology training at Montefiore Medical Center in Bronx, N.Y. says that separation anxiety and procrastination are two of the leading causes of clutter. In addition, he says most clutter can be traced to cognitive errors in thinking. "We all have these dysfunctional thoughts. It's perfectly normal," Dr. Rego says. The trick, he says, is to recognize the irrational thought that makes you cling to an item and substitute one that helps you let go, such as, "Somebody else could use this, so I'll give it away." (Beck, 2014) Sentimental objects and things that are sometimes called "chotchkies" are the most common things that are psychologically difficult to dispose of. Author Barry Dennis even went as far as to create something called the "Chotchky Challenge" where he challenged disorganized people to get rid of their "chotskies," a word that comes from the Yiddish word "tchotchke," referring to a trinket or knickknack. Dennis expands that definition and instead uses it to refer to pretty much anything that takes up space and doesn't serve a relevant purpose. Some surprising chotchkies that Dennis brings up are things like electronic equipment that keeps us from living in the moment; people who are emotionally draining; CDs and DVDs that are not used regularly; junk food and unwanted or unloved gifts from people that you probably don't even care about. (Dennis, 2012)

So, think about the psychology of who you are as a disorganized or cluttered person, deal with that emotional adversary, get rid of your unnecessary chotchkies, and prepare to live the zen life of an organized person. You can start like I did in the bathroom at my house. Go into your office and make three piles: Keep, Trash, and Sell. You can have a garage sale or donate to Good Will the items that might still be useful to someone else but that you don't need. Donate to Salvation Army, Goodwill or the SPCA. Once you have gotten rid of some unnecessary items you can begin to lay out your ideal office and will be on the fast track to organization.

Chapter 3 – OFFICE PLANNING AND DESIGN

"What we imagine is order is merely the prevailing form of chaos." Kerry Thornley

What does your office say about you? Are you neat and organized, logically placing things where they will provide the most use or are you comfortable, assuring others that you know where everything is even though it looks like a cluttered mess to the naked eye? Maybe you just work wherever you can find an open space and don't even have a defined area for your office. Well, let me tell you, those things are slowing you down and lowering your ability to achieve great things and secure efficient productivity! Clutter is production's kryptonite! On the opposite end, some of you may have everything neatly tucked away, obsessed with not having anything visible at all. Just because you have things hidden away doesn't mean that you don't have clutter. This type of person usually buys things more than once because they've stored something away and then forgot where it was or that they even purchased it.

Whether you already have a home office or you are creating an office in your home now that you've decluttered, you need a plan. Your comfort and productivity can be increased with a bit of attention to your surroundings. The encouraging news is this can be completed in 30 days or less for most of you!

Your business is an important part of your life and worth the investment of your time and funds to create the best office possible. Your office needs to be a place where you can work efficiently in order to be productive. Take a pen and paper and decide on a budget for the project. Do you need to use what you already have or do you want to upgrade? What does this look like in the budget?

When you have the budget nailed down, it is time to think about the details of creating an office custom fit for you....the entrepreneur! You can look online or in magazines to get an idea of what style of office that you might like. Print or cut some photos out and compare them so that you have a clear focus of what kind of office will be a calm, productive retreat for you.

LOCATION AND ORIENTATION

Where is the best place for you to work? A place that is private and quiet. Do you need to work undisturbed? Frequent interruptions will interfere with your work. Every time you are interrupted, it takes about five minutes to focus and get back to where you left off. If that happens only 6 times during the day, it translates to 30 minutes of wasted time in one day. Multiply that times 5 days a week! Those minutes add up fast.

When working at home, especially if children are present, it may be tempting to work in the middle of the activity. However, a few minutes of distraction may actually take hours away from your focus and creativity. It can be more productive to schedule specific times when you will be available, similar to taking scheduled breaks at a corporate job. Children will have the assurance of time spent together with you and your work time will benefit from being able to concentrate for longer periods of time.

Of course, *only you* can decide what place works best for you. If you are working from home so that you can supervise the children, you will need to be closer to the activity so you can supervise! If you are having a challenge in completing your work and you have children that need supervision, perhaps you can hire someone to watch them for a few hours. If money is tight, then you might trade with someone for time or services. Maybe you could schedule a play date with another parent. This is a situation where you can use your creative energy to find a solution that benefits everyone. The children may welcome the break, too. You can also try something that I call entertain and contain! Create a schedule so that you can focus on the work that requires more concentration around nap time or when the pitter patter of little feet have left the house to visit grandma or the sitter. If you aren't comfortable with a napping child in a different room, utilize a porta-crib so that you can get the most out of your quiet time.

CLIMATE CONTROL

A comfortable temperature is a big plus for me. It is hard to be effective when you are freezing or hot. You might add a small heater or additional cooling source if the temperatures are a problem in your home office. The room for my home office is in the back of the house and in the winter, it can be really cold in the corner I chose for my desk. However, with the assistance of a small infrared heater that problem is resolved. I just shut the door and turn on the heater.

Is there a location where you will be away from family activities so that you can work undisturbed and be comfortable? That might be a good place for your office. Do you have a space that will not be disturbed by routine family activities? It can be tempting to stop what you are doing and join in the fun, but save it until you have completed your goals for the day. After you have experienced the satisfaction of finishing tasks and projects without interruption, you can decide if the concept works well for you.

Even if you are the only one in your home during business hours, set a schedule for the day and stick to it. If you were at a job you would have expectations for your work hours. Do you have set business hours? You can post the times you are available on your website along with a notice that you are also available by appointment at other times.

There is a method called the Pomodoro Effect. It was created by Francesco Cirillo in the late 1980's. It is a concept of working for short intervals of time and then taking a scheduled break. These intervals are known as "pomodori", plural for the Italian word "pomodoro" for "tomato". He named the technique after the tomato-shaped kitchen timer that he used. This concept teaches you to work with time instead of struggling against it. Divide your time into segments where you will concentrate on a single task and then take a scheduled break. His suggestion is thirty minutes. Work for 25 minutes without interruption and then take a five minute break. If you think of other ideas or thoughts during the 25 minutes, write them down on a notepad and bring your attention back to what you are working on. This accomplishes two things. You get time specifically assigned to the task but do not lose the idea that came to mind because you wrote it down on the notepad. If you don't write down the thought, it keeps circling in your mind and interrupts your concentration. As other ideas come, add them to the notepad and continue with what you were doing. This may sound simplistic, but it works.

In the beginning, I tried to just ignore the random thoughts but they just brought their friends and became another form of clutter that was distracting to me. I spent more time trying to ignore the ideas than it took to jot them down on paper. So, take a pen and paper and divide the hours you plan to work into thirty minute segments. List what you need to get done and the time it should take to finish each. For example, if you are making customer contacts, how long should that take? In an hour, you would make the calls for 25 minutes and then take a five minute break. Then come back and call for another 25 minutes before the next 5 minute break. Sometimes when you work from home, people assume that you are always available. You have to remember that you are working and phone calls and emails should be treated the same as if you were in a business office.

If you are interrupted by the phone or email, ignore it and keep on with your scheduled task. You can listen to the message or return the call during your 5 minute break. Maybe you could schedule a play date with the children of another parent. Need to do a load of laundry? Put the clothes in the washer during your break and come back to put them in the dryer during a subsequent break. As a friend once told me – *"Don't knock it until you try it"*.

You don't need to schedule your entire day like this, but it helps productivity to do it on a regular basis. I like scheduling four hour blocks a couple times a week. For me, it helps to have a set time to work on projects during the week. The result is a measurable product and I have results that I can measure.

I have found that using this simple technique has enabled me to finish major tasks by the end of the day. When I started using the method, I discovered that I had been fragmenting my work time into so many segments that I was wasting time and not getting work or things such as the laundry completed. I also put time slots into my schedule where I am at liberty to do whatever needs to be done. If I need to make calls, write notes or do research; that still works well within the Pomodoro framework.

Cirillo developed an entire concept of time management using a simple kitchen timer. Feel free to use a digital timer or even the one on your phone to track your minutes and remain focused.

It's all about the space

Options may be limited because of responsibilities but choose the room that gives you the best location for your comfort and productivity if it is possible. Even though you are working in the home, it needs to be treated as a business if you want to get the best return on your investment of time and effort. Make sure that you have the best lighting and reliable internet reception.

If you need to work without interruption, having your own drinks and a snack may encourage you to keep at the project and make real progress in a single day. The method is simple to use and can have a big payoff when you stick with it. The idea behind all of this is to create a work/ life balance that helps you live the life you desire. You may not have many options, but choose the room that gives you the best location for your comfort and productivity.

One of my favorite perks from a home office is being able to abandon it and head down the hall to the den or kitchen. You can take a break from the routine tasks and work off a table or counter so you can take a mental break in addition to stretching your legs out for a rest. When I have had colleagues working together at my house for a project, we gathered around the kitchen table and propped our computers up and started to work.

A lot can be accomplished in a casual setting and it is good to have a change of scenery and conversation as you collaborate with others. Are you scheduled for a conference call? Find a place where you can sit back and relax and yet the work gets finished. With Wi-Fi, it is possible to work almost everywhere. Enjoy your home office but be more productive than in a regular office with a commute and distractions.

Orientation

As you think about where you will place your desk, notice how the light comes into the room. Is there a view you would like to have? How about traffic and noise? If there is a lot of traffic or distraction below the window, you may not want to have your view be that of the passersby.

In my home office I have a view that looks out on the garden and I can see the flowers and watch the birds and squirrels chasing each other around the backyard. It is not distracting to me. In fact, I find that it is actually peaceful. It does not seem like I am toiling away at my desk if I can get a glimpse of the outside activities.

If the only view you have is of traffic, you may want to turn your back to the windows and face the interior. Distraction is a form of clutter and breaks your concentration. Personally, I am not able to watch television and get much done. The same applies to a diversion such as traffic. Consider your choices and make a decision so you can work effectively.

If you are undecided about where to place the furniture, try actually moving the desk and chair around the room and sitting for a few minutes to find the spot where you have the best lighting, reception and air control.

Chapter 4 - CREATE A PLAN FOR FURNITURE

"He who lives in harmony with himself lives in harmony with the universe."— *Marcus Aurelius*

When you were in school, did you follow the instructions when directed to create an outline before you start a major paper or did you skip the outline and just started right? How did that work out for you?

I will admit that often I did not take the time to create the outline and the results were sometimes less than my best work; however, I learned from that experience that a plan is worth the time and effort that it requires. Please take this word of advice and take pen and notebook in hand and start on your plan.

What are some of the items required for you to work effectively? That list probably includes things like a desk and chair, additional seating, a light, a bookcase, additional workspace, and storage.

Draw a diagram of your floor plan and experiment with different furniture arrangements. Does a U-shape arrangement work for you? How about a T- shape or a single desk? A desk can also be made by bringing two rectangle tables together in an L shape. This arrangement gives flexibility that allows you to modify for different projects. In choosing the layout, consider the size of the room and the work to be done.

If you are making a furniture or equipment purchase, take the room measurements with you and decide how you would place it in the room before you purchase. It is a real problem if you get the desk and it is too big. Returning a desk would be a real hassle!

What about your chair?

It is all about the chair! Since most office work requires long hours of sitting in a chair, it puts stress on the spine and hip area S. You do not want to develop or worsen back problems. Sitting improperly puts stress on the spine and hip areas. It is much easier to prevent pack pain than to cure it. You need a chair that encourages good posture and supports the lower back.

When you sit in your chair, sit up straight, but not rigid. Your ears shoulders and hips should be in a vertical line. When sitting for long periods, you can lean forward, keeping your alignment and in a few minutes shift back in the seat to relieve stress on your spine. The ideal chair should fit the curve of your back and allow for easy movement.

The US government site states:

"Ergonomics is the scientific study of people at work. The goal of ergonomics is to reduce stress and eliminate injuries and disorders associated with the overuse of muscles, back posture, and repeated tasks. This is accomplished by designing task, workspaces, controls, displays, tools, lighting, and equipment to fit the employee's physical capabilities and limitations."

There are many selections of ergonomic chairs. Test several different styles for the best fit before selecting. As people have become aware of the big difference the right chair makes, sales have increased quickly. These are designed for height and size of the individual using it. The arm rests and even seat depth can be customized for comfort. As I spend most of my time seated at the desk, the chair is probably my most important investment in furniture.

If you are choosing a desk, even those are adjustable these days. Standing to work is becoming popular. I recently toured a company where employees have desks that can be raised to stand or lowered to work seated. Each person had created a work space that was just right for them. Some were standing and working on projects that needed movement about the area. Others had created a regular seating arrangement and were working diligently at their computers.

It was interesting to see how they customized their work stations. The employees could choose how they would work. This option actually allowed more activity to be going on at the same time. Our tour guide talked about how productivity had increased along with employee participation and innovation. Their employee retention was also increased. The employees were having fun and getting work done. I am putting an adjustable desk on my want list for the future so I can keep my regular desk and add an adjustable alongside. Then I could multi-task instead of feeling locked into position. I have also seen some homemade solutions that work well.

Recently, I was in a client's home office and her husband had created a shelf for his computer so he can stand to work. As I worked there for a couple of hours with my computer, I found it easy to stand and type. Mobility was not restricted as we worked on a website project.

If you want to try something different, take a standing desk for a test drive. Does standing to work interest you? Before investing in a new desk, work off the top of a bookcase or table it to see how it feels. You could be pleasantly surprised and find it works for your comfort. Be sure that you utilize things like drawer dividers and customizers so that you can organize your drawers and are not just shoving things into the drawers.

Chapter 5 - THE POWER OF FOCUS

"Our behavior is governed by principles. Living in harmony with them brings positive consequences; violating them brings negative consequences." - Stephen R. Covey

If you find yourself doing the same thing every day, switch your workplace and put some variety in your work. We rush to meetings and multitask at every opportunity. It creates a false sense of success and we do not realize that we are actually wasting time instead of gaining time. Combining technology with our fast pace of living causes stress and loss of focus. Let's talk about why focus is important.

In life today, we seem to be busier than ever before. We have more tools that give us more to do but no time to do it. Do you feel a sense of stress and overwhelm? The "time management" just adds more stress to our lives as it suggests there are other ways to cram even more into busy schedules and cluttered lives. It seems if we don't multitask every minute of the day we are not productive. That is not true.

The people that I know that are super productive, excel in being focused. What are you doing and saying that is not essential? Are you wasting time and resources rushing to do things that are not really important? Learning to be focused and on task will increase what you achieve because you will do it in a conscious way that is planned and has structure and form. At the end of the day, you will have an increased sense of fulfillment that you can measure. In the following pages, you'll learn tips on how to gain and keep your focus while increasing your productivity in all you do. In my experience, multitasking is overrated. Let's look at why multitasking doesn't work and develop ideas to do instead. This is sound appealing? I invite you to read on.

The Importance of Focus

What happens when you are focused? Do you notice less stress? Do you have more joy in your life? Why don't people focus more? It is an important skill to learn to focus. Maintaining focus for a definite period of time enables you to work faster and be more creative. One task at a time is enough stress on your mind and being less stressed increases happiness.

There many reasons that it is hard to remain focused on one project for very long. In today's world we are surrounded by phones, television, radio, social media, and an ever-increasing population in our towns and cities. It has become difficult to get time for yourself and to maintain your personal space.

John B. Calhoun was noted for his behavioral research on the effects of population density and effects on behavior. He claimed that the effects of overpopulation on rodents were a model for the future of the human race. In his studies, Calhoun created the term "behavioral sink" to describe behaviors in overcrowded population density studies and "beautiful ones" to describe passive individuals who withdrew from all social interaction. He presented his findings at conferences around the world and was sought out by groups concerned with overcrowding in local jails and prisons and lectured on how the effects of overcrowding would influence future population growth.

Calhoun taught at Emory University and Ohio State University. The professor worked on the road and ecology project at John Hopkins University. In 1947 he began a 28 month study of a colony of Norway rats in a 10,000 square-foot outdoor pen. He observed how the rats organize themselves in colonies of a dozen rats each. By studying their organization techniques, Calhoun determined that 12 rats is the maximum number that can live harmoniously as a natural group. After that, stress and psychological effects functioned to break up the group. I will spare you the more gory details of how the rats failed to function as a society when their numbers increased and they were crowded together.

Do you see how this could apply to the effects that our busy lives have on our relationships and productivity?

When I was in the corporate world, I had a supervisor that prided herself on being able to multitask constantly. When someone in our group would enter her office and attempt a conversation, she hardly looked up to see who was there. I remember having conversations with her where her response did not even relate to what I was discussing. When the topic would come up in a later conversation, she would swear it had never been mentioned.

It became such a problem with our group that we finally escalated our concerns. When she finally transferred to another location, our morale and effectiveness improved dramatically. Even today, when I think of multitasking, she immediately comes to mind. In order to get away from increased levels of a distraction, find a room where you can close the door and turn off your phone and email.

Focus Factor #1

When you are away from distractions, your brain can focus on a single task. By avoiding distractions, you to complete the project more quickly that you would have if you had tried to do more than one task at a time. For example, when you're trying to write a blog post, catch up on your bookkeeping for the week or even research information for a speech, working on a single thing enables you to give all your attention to the task at hand. Turn off the television and silence your cell phone. Stop all those pings that divert your attention!

Focus Factor #2

When you give focus to the task without all the distraction, it goes more quickly and has fewer mistakes. The quality of your work will improve as well. Creativity increases and you can come up with new ideas related to what you're doing instead of being constantly distracted by random thoughts constantly coming to mind.

If you are an artist, writer, designer, musician even a photographer who needs new ideas, lack of focus means you will not get as much work done. Also, you will not be as effective.

The distraction of being constantly in contact with others takes away focus and increases your stress in addition to diminishing productivity. If you are truly focused on the task at hand, much more would be accomplished.

Take time to focus on one thing at one time for a period of time. Scattering your thoughts over multiple tasks at once keeps you distracted from what you need to be doing. Being focused means you can complete your task quickly and move on to the next. If you are trying to remember everything you need to do at the same time - your thoughts are scattered and little gets accomplished.

Let your subconscious do the work. Think about how you learned to ride a bike or drive a car. In the beginning it was difficult but as you focused and concentrated your mind took over and helped you learn. It's the same in your everyday life. Focusing on one task at a time enables your subconscious to help you work faster and easier.

Focusing on a single task increases productivity and quality of your work as you are less stressed. Gaining focus translates into increased creativity and happiness.

Focus Factor #3

Multitasking is like a sheep in wolf's clothing. It appears as one thing but turns out to be something much different. If you are like most, you are so accustomed to multitasking that you are not even aware that of it. Many employers look for that skill in their employees. The misconception is widely spread that multitasking saves time. Multitasking is bad and there are many reasons to explain why. Being focused is better. It lets you concentrate on one thing at a time, instead of thinking about every task. It helps create better results in less time.

Do you multitask because you become bored working on just one thing at a time? What is wrong with multitasking?

Because you have to switch from task to task, your mind has to switch back and forth between thoughts and directions. It requires you to stop and take time to remember what you're doing.

Attention and memory loss are one of the effects of multitasking. Professor Clifford Nass published his findings in the proceedings of the National Academy of Science. He reported that those who use social media online and multiple forms of electronic communication have trouble focusing on their tasks and receive lower scores on memory tests.

There is evidence of diminished cognitive performance. Zheng Wang, a professor at Ohio State University, observed that when students multitasked, they felt more productive but were actually reducing cognitive skills and abilities such as studying. When you multitask as you interact with others, it is perceived as rude. It is often that those who multitask find themselves in contact with others. When you only pay half attention to someone as you answer texts and phone calls while talking to them, you lose their respect.

Productivity is lost by multitasking. When you switch between tasks, it decreases productivity and concentration. Time is lost as you change to a different task. A project is less likely to be finished by multitasking. The task finished for the day will be a lower quality that if focus had been on one project to completion.

When multitasking, it is difficult to focus entirely on a single task. As you think about emails you had to respond to while you were writing a report with the phone ringing continuously, your mind creates a list of things to do and cannot concentrate on the task at hand. Working this way doesn't accomplish anything other than causing you stress. You should prioritize your tasks instead of multitasking among several. Maintain your focus by breaking a project into working sections of time.

Chapter 6 – KEEP YOUR FOCUS

"Successful people maintain a positive focus in life no matter what is going on around them. They stay focused on their past successes rather than their past failures, and on the next action steps they need to take to get them closer to the fulfillment of their goals rather than all the other distractions that life presents to them." -Jack Canfield

So, you want to focus on one task but find yourself being distracted. Sometimes it is difficult to focus on the task at hand because your mind wanders. You worry about other things or maybe you have too many things you need to do to focus on one task. The following tips will help you find your focus.

Take Time to Meditate

As you begin your day take at least 30 minutes to meditate. If you don't feel you have 30 minutes, you can still take a short period of time and focus. As you focus on breathing really concentrate on the air as you breathe in. How does it feel as it crosses your lips? What is the feeling as the air escapes? In the beginning, your mind will wander and fill your head with constant thoughts. As this happens, bring your mind back to focus on your breathing. Practice this for several minutes each morning and soon you will master the technique.

As you regulate your breathing it relaxes your circulatory system and gives a sense of peace.

Listen

When you listen to music it helps improve your focus. Don't just listen but instead concentrate and focus on the music and only the music. Select a single instrument and follow it through the piece.

Break Up Goals

Having an end goal on your mind when you work on the task can be frustrating because your target is too big or difficult. You won't finish quickly and it may seem like you aren't making any progress. Break it down into smaller, more achievable goals instead of working towards the ultimate goal at the end. Make a list of smaller goals that can be reached in a few days. As you achieve each goal; cross it off your list.

Your Personal Time Clock

Learn to find your body's most comfortable time. Perhaps you work best in the morning before sunrise. Do you work better late at night? Set aside your most productive time of the day to do your work. Many authors arise early and do their writing while others are still sleeping. Other artists work best at night and fall asleep during the day.

Eat Lightly

Have you noticed that when you eat a big meal for lunch, then return work, that big meal seems to weigh on you all afternoon? Eating a meal loaded with carbohydrates makes you sleepy. Your body needs to focus all its energy on digesting all that food you just consumed. If you can go on a small juice fast on a regular basis it will help keep you alert and your body in good physical condition. Be sure that you clear any major changes in how you eat and exercise with your physician first.

Take Time to Exercise

Try to exercise your body and your mind daily. Try working a crossword puzzle or engaging in a lively discussion. When's the last time that you tried building something creative? Even a simple 30 minute walk daily can help maintain your focus as you keep your body healthy.

Push Yourself

When you're feeling lazy, it may help to push yourself to take the next action. Perhaps a mental a roadblock takes time away from the task at hand. Do something else until you can regain your focus and concentrate on the original task.

Learning to improve your focus takes a little time but yields big rewards. Start by trying a couple of these tips each day. As you begin to change habits notice how well and quickly you can become focused.

It is surprising how many people lose track of where time goes. It may seem like they are focused on a single task, but are they? Try completing this list to see how you spend your time for an entire week. You may find that you have been wasting time on little things like checking email or Facebook or even sending a few tweets every hour.

To increase focus and productivity, try some of the strategies.

1. Keep track of your time. After a week analyze the results. Determine where you can eliminate time wasters.

2. Start your week with a plan. When the week has ended, find a quiet place where you will not be interrupted and make a list of key projects for the coming week. Note the tasks that are associated with them. Be certain to add in activities with friends and family that you participate in they will not be overlooked.

3. List the projects of the new week in order of importance. Begin with the most important and continue until you have listed the least important. Use a calendar to chart blocks of time so that you will not be interrupted. Schedule anywhere from 15 to 60 minutes to work on each task. The amount of time scheduled will vary with the complexity of the task.

4. Review your list and remove what is not essential. Are there things that you need to do that could be outsourced? Outsourcing doesn't have to be a technical job. It can be something as simple as mowing the yard or going to the grocery store. Hiring a virtual assistant to do your social media for the week can add hours of productivity time at a minimal expense.

5. Write down your goals. For the big or long term goals, divide them into smaller weekly or daily ones. It makes them easier to focus on.

6. Mark down a specific time of the day when you will check and answer emails and interact with social media. Perhaps you want to do this for about 30 minutes at the beginning of each day and then you can do the same at day's end. At lunch you might schedule time to handle personal business. If you attempt doing these things in the middle of a task it completely stops your productivity and interrupts your concentration and focus and thus creates more of a problem than just the loss of a few minutes.

7. Eliminate multitasking. It will take practice to learn how to focus on just one project at a time. If you will stick with it and learn the discipline of only doing one task at a time, it will become a habit. It will be a habit that will have great returns on how much you accomplish during the day. Maintain a laser focused intensity on just one thing at a time. Productivity will soar.

8. Establish a parking lot list. It is so easy to become distracted because we want to look something up. It doesn't take but just a minute to do a search on the internet. We think *"I wonder if anything has been added to my Facebook feed? Who was that actor we saw in the movie last week? I wonder if anything*

interesting is going on at the zoo tomorrow". Each of these ideas is a distraction and takes about 25 minutes of concentration away from my work. By the time I research every idea that comes into my head, productivity is diminished. Instead, write the thought on a piece of paper (even better, use Evernote. Can you tell I love Evernote?).

9. Just say no. When today's task list is full, don't be tempted to take on a project for someone else. *"No"* can be a very productive word when said in an appropriate way.

10. Establish an environment that works for you. Do you need quiet space away from people telephones and television noise? Establish your office space so that it works for you. Include decorations that are soothing. Use soft colors, inspirational artwork, and even that comfortable chair we talked about. If you work best in an area that is clean and neat, be sure to put away papers and magazines before starting. Do you focus better while listening to music or some kind of background noise? Then add that to your office environment.

11. When you need a break, take one. As I mentioned before about the Pomodoro method, short breaks decrease boredom and prevent burnout when you are trying to concentrate on the big project. Walk around

the room stretch your legs, even jog in place. Circulate your blood and you will feel better and be more alert.

12. Chunk tasks into smaller more manageable sections of time. Short breaks can be scheduled as I discussed earlier and then you can take five minutes as a break. Come back to your task and work for another 25 minutes followed with a five minute break. Continue this way for a couple of hours. Now it's time to take a longer break so that you can relax and return refreshed to the project you are working on.

13. Take a thirty minute break and do something that is not related to what you have been doing.

14. The new smart phones have apps that can help with productivity and concentration. Evernote can help keep you organized by helping eliminate distractions. Download it or another app like Brainwave where you can choose settings like "concentration boost" and "problem solving", "brainstorming", or "creative thinking". Other apps are out there to help you stay focused and productive during the day.

Focus Improving Exercises

When Diane Sawyer was asked the secret for her success, she replied that there is no substitute for paying attention. Were you aware that you can improve your focus by practicing simple exercises? It's the truth. Simple things such as getting exercise daily and chewing gum can help improve brain function, leading to better focus. Most focus exercises can be completed in less than ten minutes.

Try these exercises to get started:

1. Mutter under your breath to yourself. This would certainly have gotten me in trouble when I was younger. This might seem crazy but talking to yourself out loud can increase your attention span, calm you emotionally and tell you how to act.

2. Do you drink caffeine in order to boost your concentration? This works, but may create a lack of focus when you are not caffeinated. Have you ever felt your energy spiral downward as the caffeine wears off? Try physical exercise to increase your focus. Exercising triggers the release of brain chemicals that affect our learning and memory, which are what help us focus.

3. Stay hydrated. Even slight dehydration increases distraction. A 2% dehydration level can affect and decrease your ability to concentrate on cognitive activities.

4. Get plenty of sleep. At least seven hours of good quality sleep is required nightly to help your body and mind rejuvenate and leads to better concentration and focus during the day.

5. Count backwards from 100 to 0. I found this very effective. I certainly could not think about anything else while doing this, even though it was easy.

6. Imagine a scene in your mind and name the colors you see, or count the waves as you imagine yourself on the seashore.

Are you still having difficulty concentrating? If you have ever participated in meditation, you are probably instructed to pick a word or sound and repeat it softly to yourself for at least five minutes. Try doing this on a regular basis and increase the time as you learn to do it effectively.

Try visualization. Shut your eyes and focus on an image with your entire mind. Imagine yourself sitting on a beach in the sun. Can you hear the waves lapping against the shore? Practice this image or something similar until you can hold that thought in your mind for at least five minutes.

If you will make this practice a part of your daily routine, you will find an increased ability to focus and concentrate on what you need to do during the day.

Do you have focus issues?

I am sure you already know how difficult it is to maintain focus on a single thing. This is often the result of things like boredom, lack of interest or physical or mental fatigue. It can also be affected by our motivation and interest in the task.

Vitamins like the B complex group, biotin, or Vitamin H and lettuce are reported to help improve memory. When you eat the right foods it helps with focus and brain health. It is reported that foods such as meat, beans, oranges, nut butters and oysters may increase brain health. Make certain that you don't have allergies to any of these foods before you consume them.

If you still find that you can't focus on one thing for any length of time, check with your doctor. There are several conditions, such as depression, that can cause a lack of focus. Your doctor can rule out any physical cause that relates to your lack of focus.

When you're working on your computer to complete a project, close any tabs that are not related to what you're doing. Closing those tabs keeps you from being distracted by the temptation to check out all that fun information that seems to pop up from nowhere.

Create a list of tasks online, things that you do on a regular basis. If you will schedule a regular time for checking your email and social media each day and it will diminish distractions and increase productivity.

Set aside time in your day for creativity, leaving additional segments for work and communication in addition to time for yourself. Divide the day up however it works best for you.

Constantly dealing with focus issues affects your productivity. As distractions mount, focus declines. You may also find ways to control focus problems through diet, exercise and establishing regular exercise habits.

Chapter 7 – APPLY YOUR FOCUS

"I've discovered that my definition of 'having it all' is really: Enough. Enough time to attend most of my boys' school events, enough challenge at work that it matters and enough time that I can make choices about what balance means -- to me -- each and every day." Anne Rohosy

It is possible to increase your productivity and do more in less time with a technique called Applied Focus. It can help you avoid the little distractions that can take away productivity.

Applied Focus is a technique that helps you multiply your efforts. Each session is 45 minutes and contains a 15 minute shift in focus. You can also do a 90 minute session with a 30 minute shift that follows on focus. In other words, concentrate intently on your task for the 45 or 90 minute session and switch to something completely different for the break in focus. In the focus session however, don't allow any distractions that are not a real emergency. No phone calls, emails pinging, texting or Facebook. All are off-limits.

Here are some ideas that may help:
1. Only open one browser or application at a time. If you are writing a blog post, only Word or your notepad is open.

2. Time your sessions. Don't go over your 45 or 90 minute session, no matter how focused you are. The break is necessary.

3. Step away from your task. Move away from your desk, move around, go for a drink or snack. Take a brain break.

4. Prepare ahead of time. Separate the research task or session from the focus session that includes the writing. That way, you can concentrate on just the writing or the research.

5. Schedule a session for email, telephone and social media.

6. Applied Focus sessions can be a game changer if you use them.

7. Plan ahead for a reward to give yourself when your sessions are finished. This can be as simple as a walk outside or a trip to the café near your home.

8. Make a list of things that you want to accomplish and post it near your desk. As you complete individual parts, check those tasks off your list. This gives you a visual reminder of what you are accomplishing.

9. When possible, do the things that you like least first so they will not be looming before you but will be instead be checked off the list! Done! Task completed!

This technique is simple but not to be underestimated. It's the simple tips that can make big changes in how you perform in your business. If what you are currently doing is not meeting your goals, test this idea and you may be pleasantly surprised. I am using the same technique to write this book. After I complete this next section, I shall go for a walk. What do you have to lose? You have much to gain.

Applied Focus sessions may increase your productivity but may take some adjustment. Change slowly. Schedule one or two sessions a day until you become accustomed to the routine. Soon you will notice improvement in your concentration and productivity.

What's next?

Learning to focus on one task at a time takes time and commitment. In our busy lives we are pulled in many directions at once. Begin your journey to a more focused life slowly by implementing tips and strategies found within this report. Focus is an important part of productivity. You'll be more productive in a shorter time than you have been if you can focus on one task for a set amount of time. Multitasking may be tempting, but put that aside for now. Soon you will be able to finish one project before moving on to another.

Create an environment where you are comfortable - one that fits with how you work. Removing distractions can improve focus and increase productivity. Are you a morning person? If so, focus on your work task first thing in the morning. The same is true for night owls.

Healthy and nutritious foods help to keep your brain strong and able to concentrate. When you exercise daily, meditate and take time to enjoy nature and your family, you will have achieved a healthy work-life balance. Whether or not you live alone, distractions are around every corner. Learning to delay interruptions and remain on task makes better use of your time, gives you a sense of power over your work and can increase your available time for having fun.

THE 30 DAY PLAN

DAY 1

Start with a quick pass to clear out the clutter. Do you have boxes piled in a corner with files that you have not used in years? 1. What are you required to keep for documentation such as taxes or legal resources? 2. Is there a better place to store it? 3. How much space do you have for storage in your office? Now is the moment to decide...eliminate what is not necessary and find space for the rest. If overflow is essential, you can store in garage, attic or rent additional storage space. Another option is to store digitally and keep a backup in a separate place for security of essential documents. Sort into three boxes: Keep, Toss and Recycle or Sell

DAY 2

Finish the clutter purge from yesterday. Put the Keep box aside and then find best place for those items when your office furniture is in place. Plan the lighting, outlay of the room and clear out storage areas and remove what goes away. Arrange items in the keep box from yesterday and put in place what you can. If you are interested, look online for adjustable desks. Some are free-standing and others can be placed on top of a table. I will have examples of those on my website. You can also improvise and see if you like how it feels to work standing up. I found it a good way to break the monotony of sitting for hours at a desk. I am planning to add one to my office setup soon. I will still sit much of the time, but enjoy the freedom of standing and moving about the room also.

DAY 3

Go through magazines, books and decide what to keep and what is not business related and can be put somewhere else. If these have been laying around and just piling up - then seriously consider how they could be better used by someone else. You can take magazines and give away or put somewhere such as nursing homes, hospitals or even take to the doctor's office and leave (with their permission, of course). I always cut out my information if it is on the label. When you sit down to watch TV or visit with the family, this would be a good time to multi-task and go through paperwork at the same time.

DAY 4

AT the beginning of the week (Sunday night for most) take out your planner and plan your coming week. Write down what you are going to do on this project day by day and give it a time and place in your written schedule. When planning your week - what can you delegate or not do yet? If it is not income producing, consider moving it to another time when you are not working on an important project (and this is an important project) Plan appointments and meetings and put them on your calendar so none are missed. Review your plans for the week and add in time for product creation, marketing and networking.

DAY 5

Make a plan for handling mail. What will you do with the mail as you enter the house? (tossing it on the kitchen counter is not the best answer) Make yourself a written note so you can refer to it until it becomes a habit. When you get your office set up ..include a set of baskets and label them IN and OUT. As you come into the office with the mail, open it close to the trash can and recycling bin. Deal with it as soon as possible. If a quick call will solve a problem, make it right away instead of going back and forth on emails. Stop the junk mail. On the back of most catalogs there is an 800 number to remove you from their list. To lessen junk mail - write to: Mail Preference Service, Direct Marketing Association, P.O. Box 9008, Farmington, N.Y. 11735-9008 - to stop catalogs go to https://www.catalogchoice.org/login - also CatalogChoice.org and DMAchoice.org You will not see instant results, but in about 60 days you should notice a difference.

DAY 6

Set up a filing system for paperwork. Keep your home/personal documents separate from your business files. A sturdy filing cabinet and hanging files are the backbone of your office document system. Decide if you are going to separate into types of documents or use a simple alphabetical system.

How you set up your system is not as important as how you use it. It is important to decide on the system and use it consistently. A list of categories and how filed can be posted on the side of the cabinet for easy reference. As you continue to sort through the paper in your office, take time to file it away.

DAY 7

Weekend Assignment: Purge the paper. This is a good time to multi-task while enjoying watching television - yes even while watching your favorite sports! Go through the paperwork you have set aside while clearing out your files and piles this week. Decide what to keep and file and what to trash. If paperwork contains sensitive information, set aside in a separate container and label "SHRED". Note a day and time next week to take to shredder or to outsource that task to a trusted person. You can "Google" to find a location near you. Most of the larger office supply places provide shredding services for a fee. Drop off at a secure place or watch as the documents are shredded. Your bank may offer the service as a "perk". An alternative is to buy a shredder for use in your office and shred it yourself. You may have someone in your home that can be employed to do it for you. Please remember to do it safely.

DAY 8

Shop for what you need. If you are going to replace any of the office furniture this is a good time to select what you need and arrange for delivery. Confirm that you have the necessary supplies for setting up an organized filing system. You need a sturdy filing cabinet and hanging files and folders for it. I have recently learned about some new styles of folders that are designed specifically for filing that have erasable tabs. Do you make presentations to clients? Try out some of the new multi-pocket presentation folders - some even have a special slot for a CD and your business card. If you don't have proper lighting, be on the lookout for what you need. If you strain your eyes, you may regret it later when you get a headache or blurred vision.

DAY 9

Set everything up. Put your desk and chair in place then set up the printer where you can get to it easily. Store the paper and ink supplies close by. The trash can and recycle bin can be under your desk if there is room. If not, off to the side within easy reach. Put your phone where you can use it without strain, but where it is not in the way when you are working on the computer or writing at your desk. A USB headset is desirable if you are making recordings as it does not pick up the sound of the internal computer fan. If you talk on the phone for long periods of time during the day, you may want to invest in a wireless headset for the phone. If you do not have a landline you may benefit from having a stand for your cell phone and a headset for that.

DAY 10

It is time for another planning session. Again, Sunday
night seems to be the best time for most. If you still use a paper
planner, sit down and write out days and times that you will
work on money making tasks. Determine how long a task
should take and mark the time out for it in color. After you
complete it - compare how long it took with the time you had
written in. Set up email alerts to remind you of appointments
the day before and if needed, an alert for the day of the event. I
like Google for email and calendar. When I write in a
commitment, I set up an alert for advance notice and I review
the calendar each evening. You may want to use your smart
phone to handle your calendar. Technology can be a wonderful
thing and the calendar is one of the best options for many of us.

DAY 11

Review how you are using your office equipment. Is your
printer connected so you can copy and scan also? Scanning a
document for filing or for sending to a client is convenient.
When you are opening your mail, deal with it as you open it.
Scanning correspondence into a document and filing may be
the answer to your desk clutter. Are you using your recycle bin
for tossing out the junk mail and excess paper that mail
creates? If you have personal information that needs to be
shredded, do it as you open the mail and handle promptly. This
may seem too easy, but when done on a regular basis,
eliminates most of the paper clutter. Don't let things grow old

sitting in the IN box...send them on their way promptly - put the OUT box to use also!

DAY 12

If you work online for business, a second computer screen is helpful. Once you have it set up and start using it, you will wonder how you managed without it. Do you use a laptop in your business? A docking station can turn that laptop into a convenient PC and it will clear the equipment from your working space. Do you need to lay out plans and art work so you can create and design programs or products? There are tables that expand for use and then the sides will fold down for storage. They can be stored in a corner or in a closet. Would that increase your productivity if you don't have to be constantly shuffling papers around so you can work on a project?

DAY 13

Put some thought into how you can grow your business. Do you have a website? Almost any business can benefit by putting their information online. The internet is where people go first to look for products or information. Do you have a website that you can manage yourself? A simple WordPress site can be one of the best marketing tools. If you can write a simple blog post or create a video and post to your site, you can promote your product with a minimum of expense. If you need help getting a site set up, look for someone who will set it up and then teach you how to log into it. Be sure that you own your domain name and the site outright. Do not give your money to someone who will not give you the rights to your site. If you do, then that person has control of your business. You may want to outsource the creation, but be sure to retain ownership.

DAY 14

It is time for a Focus Session. Mark off the time on your calendar and dedicate at least 4 hours to planning and content creation. Do you have a business proposal pending? Work on the outline and begin creating the project. Do you need to do research or make a call to get more information? Do it during this time. Remember to work for 25 minutes and then take a 5 minute break. (The exact number of minutes may vary, but the break is necessary so you can start maintaining Focus and increase your productivity).

DAY 15

Are you "Googling"? If you use an email address associated with a carrier such as AOL or a service provider such as a cable company, you will need to stay with them as long as you want to use their email address. If you use Gmail, it is not carrier specific. Google continues to develop technology to be your go-to resource. If you communicate with clients online, Google+ may be a no-cost alternative to conference call lines. With Google Drive, you can share specific files with an individual or group that you are working with on a project. It is also good for sending images.

DAY 16

Another Sunday night suggestion: Organize your marketing. If you post on Facebook, Twitter and Linked in - a service like Hootsuite or Social Oomph can organize your tweets and posts as you can schedule an entire month if you wish. Try to devote an hour once a week to creating your communication plan. You can pre-load the basic posts and then go in and interact personally during the week. Are you aware you can go into Facebook and schedule posts and time them for release? These tools are a big boost to productivity. I will have more specific information on my website during the coming days http://GetYourHomeOfficeOrganized.com Training and videos will be available soon.

DAY 17

Organize your networking in order to increase your contacts for business. In looking for other business people to connect with, check out Meetup.com and sign up to receive information on groups that are good resources for what you do. Visit several groups and find the ones that are active and welcoming. Take the time to get to know the people. Exchange information and schedule one-on-one sessions where you meet face to face. This is a time to get to know what their business is about - not a sales opportunity for you. Networking is about building real relationships. I am a member of two such groups and have made friends and gotten business referrals that have brought $$$ into my business. Look for a group that is outgoing and exchanges referrals on a regular basis.

DAY 18

Evernote is a must have resource for increasing productivity. From short lists to lengthy research, no matter what form your writing takes, Evernote keeps you focused on moving those ideas from inspiration to completion. Easily gather everything that matters. Clip web articles, capture handwritten notes, and snap photos to keep the physical and digital details of your projects with you at all times. Your words, images, and documents are always close at hand. Evernote's powerful search and discovery features make everything you've collected easy to find. (This information is copied directly from their website) http://Evernote.com Take time today to check it out and learn the basics. It can be a big productivity booster.

DAY 19

Set up an easy way to communicate with clients. Instead of driving a long distance or even across town, you can meet online. I like Skype and use the free version. This is a great way to connect outside regular business hours. After everyone has closed for the day, you can still be productive and work with clients around the world. If you do coaching or advice, you can connect almost anywhere ...anytime. Bring your clients to you and broaden your area of influence. The rates for calling overseas are very reasonable and cheaper than I have found with a major long distance carrier. Set aside an hour and watch a tutorial on YouTube or the website: http://Skype.com. This is a time saver and a productivity increaser!

DAY 20

What does your email say about you? Is it cluttered with information that you do not want or need? Try these tips: Unsubscribe from lists that you are not interested in. Even if you don't open them, the emails take up seconds of your time and set up computer chaos. Then if you see something interesting and open it...then that leads to another topic and so on. Soon valuable minutes or even hours can be wasted - never to be recovered. Use them for the first hour of every day to be productive. It is the best time for creativity and productivity. Don't waste it! Set up your email documents in a system just like you would do with paper files. Group documents into categories. Examples: A folder labeled CLIENTS then a subfolder that lists by name or RENTAL PROPERTY then subfolders with individual property names. How you set it up is not as important as USING IT CONSISTENTLY! Email is a time waster. Conquer email clutter and your productivity will surely increase.

DAY 21

Do you write articles for your blog or send emails and then use an auto responder service to reply to past clients? It is an excellent way to get new leads. The best source for business is a return customer. Posting content to your blog shows your clients that you are knowledgeable and current on your industry news. Today, take out your planner and write down days and times that you will create articles and emails and load them into an auto responder system for delivery. This task is one that can be outsourced.

DAY 22

Sit down and write out your marketing plan. Keeping it in your head is not a good plan. Make folders labeled Daily, Weekly and Monthly. Dedicate time this weekend to writing out a plan for each and begin to build a program for business development. As you find articles in magazines and online you will then file a copy in the folder where it can be used when the time comes to develop that topic. This saves research time and helps you focus on specific areas instead of jumping from topic to topic and not completing your goals for the day or week. Always have a file going where you can get ideas for content and marketing.

DAY 23

Do you keep getting the same questions from clients? If you have online products or ones that are physical, you will discover that some questions are asked repeatedly. Develop a list of FAQs - Frequently Asked Questions - post them on your website or support page so customers can find answers without having to wait for support to contact them. It is a big boost for customer satisfaction and saves time for you, too.

DAY 24

Declutter your email on a regular basis. This can also be done as a multi-task exercise. When you sit down in front of the television, open your laptop and begin the email purge. First, go through the files you have set up for different categories. Titles of folders could be Purchases, Doctor Info, family (with subcategories listing names) Important Info, Business Clients, Contacts, Recipes, Important Dates ...you can create the ones that apply to you. Keep the topics broad enough to cover the basics and specific enough that you can remember where you have filed needed information. After you have eliminated unnecessary information and set up the file titles, start going through your inbox and file those away. You should be able to delete many of them, especially the older ones. When you make it down to Inbox 0, it is time to do the Happy Dance. You have arrived!

DAY 25

Have you held a Pomodoro session lately? If not, get out the kitchen timer and set aside at least two hours to focus on projects that need work. Is your Social Media posted? Are your Tweets current? Set up a timed session and interact with your peers online. This is a good way to find leads. Did you know you can search Twitter for topics such as fishing and your city? If your business deals with a popular idea search for that in Facebook and Twitter, see if you can find people who are looking for what you are selling. Remember, this is a place to develop contacts and share information and ideas....that is why it is called "Social" Media. It is not called Selling Media.

DAY 26

Do you take notes from webinars and conference calls? When you are finished with the call, file those notes in a folder labeled with the date of the call and name of the event. Either track the notes online or print and save in a folder in a filing cabinet. If the information is handy, you will refer to it and be able to follow up with clients. People are impressed and appreciate when you demonstrate that you were listening and considered their issue important. When the project is completed, or the notes no longer apply, purge the system so it does not become cluttered with useless or outdated information. You will need to decide how long that is, but make a note at least twice a year to go back and clear out files.

DAY 27

Backup your website and your computer. The safest way is to have a backup done through a company such as Carbonite that is automatic and also stored away from your location. If you have your backup and your computer at the location, you could lose both in the case of a fire or water damage. Also, the backup is only as effective as the person backing it up. If your computer should crash - and this happens to almost everyone - you can buy a new one and download the stored information into it and be back in business in an afternoon. Also, have an automatic backup of your websites in addition to a backup of your important papers, such as the deed to your house. Don't leave things to chance - you may regret it.

DAY 28

Review what you have accomplished. What changes have you made in the way you organize and run your home office? Have you been able to purge paper files and organize the remainder? Is it easier to work at your desk? When you start to feel restless, make a coffee date with a colleague and share an hour or two catching up on what they have been doing. Do you have clients that would benefit from a visit? Call them and follow up with your latest project. Keep a file on customer information such as family, interests, and recent events in their life. Let them know you see them as a person, not just a client. This fosters better relationships and leads to referrals and continued business.

DAY 29

Consider outsourcing the tasks that you don't enjoy or that you don't have time to do. It does not have to be a technical task, it may be as simple as having someone in to clean house or mow the yard. If you are in charge of planning meals and entertaining the children after school, you might benefit by hiring a sitter once a week so you could focus on work. Plan your week and focus first on the things that are responsible for making money for your business. The biggest temptation for wasting productive time is email and browsing social media sites. Set a timer and keep track of the time spent so that it does not take your attention and focus away from business. This one step can double or triple your productive time.

DAY 30

Do you have things you need to learn for your business? Do you have programs you have purchased and never listened to, and certainly not mastered? When you are working in the kitchen or cleaning house, set up your laptop and listen to the training materials instead of letting them waste away on a shelf. If the information was important enough to purchase, put it to use in growing your business. When you make a purchase, log it into a spreadsheet that describes it and contains enough information that you can log in and consume the materials. I use passwords that I can remember and just put enough of it on the spreadsheet to remind me of what it is. Use a password storage system such as RoboForm or Last Pass. The first levels are free. Then you only need to remember the password for that site instead of all that you have.

Bonus Tip: One of the biggest boosts to my productivity was when I signed up for The 100 Day Productivity Challenge with Gary Ryan Blair. This program only opens up about 4 times a year. Here is my affiliate link: http://CynthiaLikes.me/AchieveGoals. I share it because it made such a difference in my ability to set goals and reach them. If you sign up, let me know and I will help encourage you. I still use the system as an alumnus.

While you are completing the 30 Day Plan, it is not necessary to do each step in order. It is important that you do learn the concepts in order starting with declutter and followed by arranging the office. Some may be done concurrently like shopping and rearranging furniture or supplies on the same days that you declutter.

Conclusion

It was the night of April 15 2012. I was watching the evening news. Imagine my surprise when a news report featured information on the tax rebate offered. I was aware of the rebate; however, I did not know that one's completed tax report had to be filed before midnight. At 10:25 that night I was startled from my chair as I realized I had about an hour and a half before I missed getting money back from the government. Now I appreciate extra money at any time but, I especially love getting money back from the government. What was I to do? The race was on!

With the help of online filing, I began to complete the necessary forms. Line after line I completed all the questions about income and deductions. Business entries, personal expenses, all the things necessary to file a complete tax return were already organized and in my documents. Imagine my excitement when I completed the entire process it about an hour. My excitement increased when I pressed the enter button and sent my tax return into IRS well before the midnight deadline. With the help of e-filing and good record-keeping, the entire process was finished.

In less than three weeks, I was pleased and excited when I received notice that my $400 was deposited in my bank account. At that moment I realized that the journey to rid myself of clutter had been a success. If it had been necessary to compile all the records that evening in less than two hours, I could not have done it. The $400 was my reward for a job well done.

I want you to have this feeling of success. Whether your home business is just beginning or if you are a seasoned professional, I hope you find tips tricks and tools that you can implement for profit and a sense of personal fulfillment.

You now have the tools at your fingertips that you can use to become a better business owner. As you work in your home business, enjoy the opportunity to be an entrepreneur. You are able to create the business of your dreams – it takes a bit of work, but then work is good for you.

The world will be a better place because you are in it. Share your vision and true self – you deserve nothing less than the best.

Don't take the shortcut – you will miss some of the adventure. Be real and be blessed- that is my wish for you.

So Sincerely!

Cynthia Charleen

http://CynthiaLikes.me/AchieveGoals

Resources

Every day brings news to my inbox of new programs and ideas to improve the internet world. No book can capture each and every thought and idea. Even if it were possible, that would amount to a mountain of clutter – and we have learned that clutter causes overwhelm.

Some of the resources I provide are affiliate links and if you purchase through them, I will receive a commission. I only recommend what I would suggest to my best friend and clients.

I have created a website where I can continue to share information that will help continue your journey to business success and productivity.

Visit with me here:

http://GetYourHomeOfficeOrganized.com

I look forward to continuing the journey with you. ~ Cynthia Charleen

Bibliography

Beck, M. (2014, July 8). The Psychology of Clutter. *The Wall Street Journal*.

Dennis, B. (2012). *The Chotchky Challenge*. Hay House Insights.

Made in the USA
Charleston, SC
07 September 2015